The **50**
Best Games for
Sensory
Perception

The 50 Best Group Games Pocket Books

The 50 Best Games for Building Self-Esteem
The 50 Best Games for Sensory Perception
The 50 Best Games for Brain Exercise
The 50 Best Games for Relaxation & Concentration
The 50 Best Games for Speech & Language Development
The 50 Best Games for Children's Groups
The 50 Best Games for Groups
The 50 Best Games for Rainy Days

The **50** Best Games for **Sensory Perception**

Andrea Erkert
translated by Lilo Seelos

HINTON**HOUSE**

Published in 2009 by

Hinton House Publishers Ltd
Newman House, 4 High Street,
Buckingham, MK18 1NT, UK

info@hintonpublishers.com
www.hintonpublishers.com

British Library Cataloguing in Publication Data
Andrea Erkert
  The 50 best games for sensory perception. – (The 50 best group games
  pocket books ; v. 5)
  1. Senses and sensation in children. 2. Perception – Study and teaching –
  Activity programs. 3. Group games
  I. Title II. Series III. The fifty best games for sensory perception
  370.1'55-dc22

  ISBN-13: 9781906531119

Originally published in German by Don Bosco
Verlag München under the title *Die 50 besten
Wahrnehmungsspiele*
© Don Bosco Verlag, München 2007

Contents

Touching Games

Breathing Games

Contents

'Man is most nearly himself
when he achieves the seriousness
of a child at play.'

– Heraclitus

Ringing Glasses

Ask the group to sit down anywhere in the room.
Choose one person to be the 'listener' and ask them to
close their eyes while you give each of the others an empty
glass and a fork. Each person then take turns to use the fork
to make their glass ring. Try to use glasses of different shapes
and sizes.

At some point, one person, who has been chosen silently
using a gesture, taps their glass twice. The 'listener' must
really concentrate and pay attention in order to recognise the
two successive sounds. As soon as they do, they should raise
their hand.

Materials

Glasses and forks

Remember & Repeat

Ask the group to sit around a table with their eyes closed. Only one person is allowed to keep their eyes open and make noises for the others to hear (for example, tapping their fingers on the table, rubbing, scratching and so on). The rest of the group have to concentrate and listen carefully.

After an agreed number of noises ask everyone to open their eyes and recall the noises they have heard in order. Alternatively, they could try to copy the noises in the correct order.

This activity exercises memory and develops finger motor skills.

Hearing a Book

This exercise facilitates auditory attention and exercises memory. Group members must be able to count from one to 20 to participate successfully in this exercise.

The group members sit comfortably in a circle of chairs and close their eyes. One person keeps their eyes open and holds a book, slowly turning one page after another and pausing after each page.

In order for the remaining group members to follow the turning of the pages, they must keep very quiet. Their task is to remember how many pages have been turned over. After a maximum of twenty pages, everyone opens their eyes and compares how many pages they think they have heard being turned over.

Timmy, Get the Ball!

Choose one person to be 'Timmy'. The task is to find a chime ball while keeping their eyes closed.

One person rolls the chime ball along the floor. In order for 'Timmy' to locate the ball, everyone else in the room must keep really quiet.

The task can be made easier if 'Timmy' is allowed to use his or her sense of touch instead of having to rely solely on their listening skills.

Materials

Chime ball or Ying Yang health ball.

Hear the Jump

Ask the group to stand in a circle with their eyes closed. One person stands in the middle of the circle and makes different noises for the others to listen to, for example, clapping their hands, clicking their fingers, stamping their feet, and so on.

At some point the person in the middle jumps once on the spot and the others have to join in and jump 'blind' as soon as they hear the sound.

How many people managed to hear the jump and join in straight away?

Who's Got the Bell?

Ask the whole group to sit closely next to each other and hide their hands behind their backs. Choose one person to leave the room.

While that person is waiting outside, place a small bell in the hands of another person in the group. They must try to keep it hidden within their hands.

Now call the waiting person back into the room and ask the person with the bell to give it a short ring. Can the guesser work out who has rung the bell?

Materials

A small bell

Recognising the Sound

Ask one person to use a fork to carefully tap a glass and various other objects and to listen to the different sounds that are produced. Encourage the 'tapper' to concentrate in particular on the high note produced by the glass. Then ask them to close their eyes.

Now ask another group member to gently tap the same objects using the fork. As soon as the person with their eyes closed thinks they have recognised the high note of the glass, they must raise their hand.

Materials

A glass
A fork
Five or six different objects: e.g., a bowl, a saucepan, a tin, a triangle, chime bars.

Whispering Names

Ask the group to stand in a circle. One person sits on the floor in the middle of the circle and whispers the name of one of the other group members. Everyone else must keep be really quiet and listen carefully, so they can hear whose name is being whispered.

If someone hears their name being whispered, they should walk quietly around the circle once. Once they have walked around the circle as quietly as possible and returned to their original place, they should sit down on the floor. The next person is sent on the same journey when they hear their name being whispered.

The exercise is complete when all group members are sitting on the floor.

Having to wait patiently in the circle until they hear their name develops the group's concentration and stamina. In addition, they will learn in a fun way to get used to silence – great practice for meditation, imaginary journeys and quiet exercises.

Hear the Hum

The group sit on chairs in a circle. One person makes some kind of humming sound while the others listen carefully. Now choose one person to wait outside the room, while five others each think of a sound (for example, clapping their hands, stamping their feet, clicking their fingers, and so on).

Then the person outside is asked back into the room and must listen to the different sounds with their eyes closed. Every now and then, the humming sound is made, which the listener must identify and indicate they have heard by raising their hand.

In addition, you could also ask the listener to try to identify and name the other sounds as they hear them.

Send & Receive

Ask the group to form pairs and stand facing each other, close together.

One person in each pair starts by saying a word (for example, tomato) using a normal volume of voice. Their partner has to repeat the word. If they repeat the word correctly, they are allowed to take one step backwards.

Then the first person says a new word, again without raising their voice, which the 'receiver' has to repeat. If they can understand and repeat this word too they can move back another step. The greater the distance between the 'sender' and the 'receiver', the more carefully the 'receiver' has to concentrate and listen and the more clearly the 'sender' has to speak.

The exercise ends when the 'receiver' has reached the other side of the room. If the 'receiver' is unable to understand a word, they should move one step closer to the 'sender' again.

Detective Sharp Eyes

Ask the group to sit on chairs in a circle. In the middle of the circle place several different items of clothing or jewellery. One person is chosen to be Detective Sharp Eyes and carefully studies the items.

Now the detective must leave the room and wait outside. One person is chosen to be the thief.

The thief chooses one of the items and puts it on. While the thief sits back down in their place, the others loudly call for help. At this cue, Detective Sharp Eyes rushes back into the room and tries to locate the stolen item.

Materials

Several different items of clothing or jewellery (for example, scarf, hat, ring, necklace, hair clip, bracelet).

Colourful String Salad

Place the differently coloured strings in a pile on the table.

After you have finished arranging the string salad, the group members have to try to locate the two strings that are the same colour and then fish them out of the string salad.

Materials

Eight or more pieces of coloured string or wool, all of the same length, two of which should be same colour.

Shoes, Shoes Everywhere!

For this activity you will need to make a set of binoculars from cardboard tubes. To do so, glue an empty match box between two toilet or kitchen roll tubes. Attach a piece of string to the binoculars so they can be worn around the neck.

Ask the group to sit on chairs in a circle and each take off one shoe and place it in the middle.

One person stands up and, using the binoculars, studies one shoe. They must then describe the shoe, using its different features, such as the colour, whether it has laces, or a heel. If someone thinks the shoe that is being described is theirs, they must raise their hand.

Materials

A home-made set of binoculars, consisting of two cardboard tubes, an empty match box and a piece of string.

Name that Leaf!

Spread out a selection of leaves from deciduous trees.

Working with the group members, choose three or four leaves, name them and describe how they are different. More able groups can select up to six leaves at a time.

Once everyone has learned the names of the leaves, send one person out of the room. While they are outside, take away one leaf. Now call the person back in, they must study the leaves and name the one that is missing.

Materials

A selection of different leaves.

Bear in the Cave

This activity requires the room to be darkened. One person waits outside the door while another pretends to be a bear and stands behind a projector screen.

Now shine the light of the projector from behind onto the screen in such a way that only the shadow of the bear is recognisable. The person outside is called back in and has to guess the name of the bear who is prowling around behind the screen.

This activity can be made more difficult by hiding two bears behind the screen.

Materials

A screen and projector, or lamp.

Mirror Action

All the group members except one stand next to each other in a row.

The remaining person is the 'mirror' and stands in front of the group. Each person in the row then takes turns to think of an action or sequence of movements, which they demonstrate in slow motion. The 'mirror' watches these carefully and then chooses one action which they to try to copy exactly.

Everyone in the row observes the 'mirror' and if someone thinks it is their action being copied they call out 'It's me!'

Dice Reaction Game

All group members sit around a table – divide into smaller groups if necessary. One person in each group shakes the cup containing the dice, places it upside down on the table and slowly lifts the cup to reveal the three dice.

Everyone watches carefully and if a six can be seen, the other group members have to react quickly and stand up from their chairs.

The last person to stand up starts the next round.

Materials

A cup and three dice – one for each group.

Assigning Colours

The group sit in a circle of chairs. In the middle of the circle there are a number of different, single-coloured objects.

One person looks carefully at all the objects before they are covered with a cloth. Another group member looks carefully under the cloth and names an object, for example, the pencil. The first person now has to try to remember the colour of that object. Was the pencil green or blue?

To check, the cloth can be briefly lifted again. Take turns for each member of the group to try to guess the colours.

Materials

Various different, single coloured objects, e.g., a building brick, a ball, a coloured pencil, a mug.

Spot the Sun

Show the group three different picture cards, displaying a sun, rain and clouds.

Next, place the picture cards face-down on the table. While the group watch carefully, move and swap the cards around for about thirty seconds. When you have finished, wink at one person who has to point to the sun card. If they choose correctly, start a new round.

Materials

Three picture cards, one showing a sun, one showing rain, one showing clouds.

Look Carefully

One person is asked to carefully observe the other members of the group walking around the room.

At a signal, everyone stands still and the observer briefly leaves the room. One of the people left in the room is wrapped in a cloak, so only their head can be seen.

The observer is called back in the room and has to try to describe the clothing that is being hidden by the cloak.

Materials

A cloak or sheet.

Intense Scents

Display a variety of food items for the group.

Ask the group members to smell the different foods and identify the item with the most intense smell as well as the item with the weakest smell.

Now ask the group to sort the items according to their intensity of smell.

Materials

A variety of food items that vary in their intensity of smell (for example, onions, garlic, milk, honey, and so on).

Beware of any food allergies in the group when selecting items.

Different People, Different Tastes

Place different items of food on plates and give each group member a spoon.

Form the group into pairs. Using the spoons, the pairs should serve each other taster portions from each plate. The person who is doing the tasting should close their eyes to help them perceive the flavour of the food more intensely.

Afterwards, the group can get together and discuss which flavours they liked best or those they didn't like at all.

Materials

Various different food items and a spoon for each person.

Beware of any food allergies in the group when selecting items.

Savour the Flavour

Increasingly, we are losing the ability to really savour a meal. Fast food and ready-made meals lead us to eat more quickly which, in turn, means that we often carry on eating even though we actually feel full. In addition, we consume too much fat and more and more people are becoming obese.

Generally, young people still have the ability to eat slowly and savour food. The following exercise can contribute to strengthening this ability, ensuring that it will not get lost.

The group sit in a circle and are each given a piece of bread. To start with, the must try to eat the bread as quickly as possible with their eyes closed.

During the second round, the children have to chew another piece of bread, this time as slowly as possible. As the bread is chewed and it softens in their mouths, they will be able to taste the flavour of the bread more consciously.

Afterwards, ask the group to open their eyes and talk about their different experiences. Encourage them to talk about the differences between fast and slow eating. They can also explore the difference between rushed and pleasurable eating using other food items.

Materials

Bread and other food items.

Taste & Fill Your Basket

Split the group into two smaller groups. Give each group a tray carrying up to twenty different food items covered with a cloth, a dice and a basket.

Each group member takes turns to roll the dice. When someone rolls a six they have to close their eyes and select a food item from under the cloth and then try to identify it through touch or taste. If they successfully recognise an item, the group is given a counter to put in their basket. If the player does not recognise the item, the next person takes their turn.

After a set time the two groups can compare results. Whose shopping basket contains the most counters?

Materials

Two sets of 20 food items, trays, baskets, cloths, dice, twenty counters per group.

Beware of any food allergies in the group when selecting items for tasting.

Smelling Spring

A meadow on a sunny spring day is a great place for discovering the first signs of spring and perhaps even seeing and hearing migrating birds returning from their winter quarters. In a meadow we don't just perceive spring using our eyes and ears, we can also smell the fresh scent of flowers and grasses.

Take the group on a spring walk and ask them to focus on what spring smells like. Encourage them to smell the different early flowers and to sense the smell of nature awakening.

After your walk, discuss what the group members smelled on their walk. Which flowers had a particularly intense smell?

Did the group only discover good-smelling things or did they also come across things that smelled unpleasant?

Tasting Water

Ask the group to pair up. Give each pair various glasses containing a selection of different juices as well as a glass of tap water. One person closes their eyes and their partner passes them different drinks to taste. The task is to identify which glass contains the tap water.

Materials

Glasses filled with different juices (for example, apple juice, orange juice, grapefruit juice) and tap water.

Search & Sniff

Ask the group to form pairs. Each pair receives a ball of cotton wool, which has been sprinkled with some drops of aroma therapy or other scented oil.

While one person in each pair closes their eyes, the other lies down comfortably on a mat or blanket and places the ball of cotton wool somewhere on their body.

The person who has their eyes closed now has to carefully crawl beside their partner's body and try to sniff out the location of the cotton wool. Once they have found the ball of cotton wool, they partners can swap roles.

This activity can contribute to reducing a fear of touch. However, if someone does not feel comfortable about participating, don't force them to join in.

Materials

Aroma therapy or other scented oils (for example, rose oil, fennel oil, mandarin oil or cinnamon-scented oil) and cotton wool.

Cocktail Mix

On a table, put out a selection of fruit juices and glasses and ask the group to sit around the table. One group member starts by choosing a partner for whom they would like to mix a cocktail.

Their partner closes their eyes and is passed a cocktail made from small amounts of two different juices. They must taste the drink carefully and try to guess the two juices the cocktail has been mixed from.

Once everyone has had a turn at mixing as well as tasting a cocktail, the group can discuss the flavours of individual cocktails.

☼ Were there cocktails that tasted particularly delicious?

☼ Were there fruit juices that did not really mix well?

Materials

Different fruit juices, one glass for each group member.

Tongue Calculator

Ask the group members to form pairs. Give each person several raisins.

One person closes their eyes and sticks out their tongue. Their partner carefully places up to four raisins on to the tongue without touching with their fingers. The person with their eyes closed must pay attention and try to sense the number of raisins on their tongue.

Regardless of whether or not they arrive at the correct result everyone is allowed to eat and enjoy the raisins!

☼ Is anyone skilled enough to sense up to 10 raisins?

Materials

Raisins

Healthy Sandwiches

On a table, put out a selection of healthy sandwich fillings that the group can use to make up their own sandwiches for lunch. To do this, each person is given a plate and some bread which they can fill using a selection of the available fillings.

Once the sandwiches have been made, all plates are put back on the table.

One at a time, the group members close their eyes and are passed a sandwich on a plate. They sample the sandwich and try to work out what is inside using only their sense of taste. Once they have guessed, they can, of course, enjoy the rest of the sandwich with their eyes open.

Materials

Wholemeal bread
Different sandwich fillings such as butter, cheese, ham, eggs, lettuce, pepper, tomato, cucumber, etc.
One plate for each person.

Beware of any food allergies in the group when selecting items for fillings.

Feel My Friend

Ask the group members to choose a partner.

Now ask them to stand opposite each other and close their eyes
and gently touch each other from head to toe.

☼ How tall is their friend?

☼ How big are their hands?

☼ What do their clothes feel like?

☼ Are they wearing glasses or jewellery?

Afterwards gather the group together in a circle. Choose one
person to be the 'guesser' and ask them to stand in the middle
with their eyes closed. Their task is to identify their partner from
a line of four people, by carefully feeling each person in the line.
If they think they have found their partner, they should stop in
front of him/her and open their eyes.

Bird of Paradise

Form the group into a standing circle. Attach several strips of coloured paper (approximately 10 cm long) to the clothes of one person in the circle.

Now ask one member of the group to stand in the middle of the circle with their eyes closed. Gently spin them around before leading them back to the others in the circle and ask them to find the 'bird of paradise' using only their sense of touch.

Materials

Coloured paper, scissors, safety pins.

Patchwork

Give each member of the group a small box containing a selection of fabric, card and paper squares with as many different textures as possible. Some fabrics can be represented more than once.

Now ask the group to close their eyes. Explain that their task is to make a patchwork pattern by laying out their squares, but in such a way that no two neighbouring squares are made from the same material. Encourage them to use only their sense of touch and carefully feel the different types of material while assembling their patchwork creation.

Materials

A selection of different types of fabric, paper and card off-cuts, cut into small squares.

Mine or Yours

Gather your group around a large table. Ask each person to place a small personal item on the table.

One member of the group starts by closing their eyes and, carefully feeling the shapes and structures of the different items one at a time, tries to find their own item. As soon as they think that they have found it, they can call out 'Mine!'

Older or more able groups, and those who have some experience with this game could be asked to assign each item they touch to its respective owner.

Materials

Personal items belonging to the group, such as a watch, a necklace, a bracelet, a hair clip, a purse, a toy car, and so on.

Sand Mountain Treasure Hunt

Ask the group to sit in a circle of chairs. In the middle of the circle, place a large bowl or tray containing a mountain made of sand. Next to it there is a pile of treasures - shells, pebbles, marbles and so on.

One at a time, ask each member of the group to go outside and then bury one 'treasure' item in the sand before calling the person back in. They now have to use their hands to burrow down into the sand and feel and name the object without revealing it.

After they have guessed, the 'treasure' can be retrieved from the sand and the next person can take their turn.

Materials

A large bowl of sand.
A selection of small objects such as shells, pebbles, marbles, and so on.

Jigsaw

Place a six-piece jigsaw puzzle on the table. Wooden jigsaws are particularly suitable, because it will be easier for the group members to feel the outline and shape of the individual pieces.

To start with, the group should have an opportunity to assemble the jigsaw while looking at the pieces.

As soon as they are able to do this without any difficulty, the second part of the exercise can begin. Ask someone to shuffle the pieces. Now ask one person to close their eyes and to try to assemble the puzzle using only their sense of touch.

Older or more able groups could try to assemble a puzzle consisting of up to 24 pieces without looking at the pieces.

Materials

A small jigsaw puzzle.

Where is the Apple?

Ask the members of the group to sit in a circle. In the middle of the circle, place a selection of objects and an apple – the same number as there are members of the group. Ask one person to carefully look at all the objects and the apple before leaving the room.

While they are waiting outside, the remaining group members choose one object each from the middle and hide it under their sweaters. Then the person outside is called back in again and has to work out who is hiding the apple by feeling the different objects through everyone's sweaters. Once they have found the apple, roles are swapped and it is another person's turn to go outside.

Materials

An apple
A selection of different shaped small objects, for example, a building block, a ball, a book, a pencil, etc.

Feel a Conker with Your Feet

Place a selection of natural items on a tray on the floor and cover with a cloth. Ask the group to sit in a circle around the items, with their shoes off.

One at a time, ask each person to close their eyes and then place the different objects under their feet.

Encourage them to feel the objects carefully using only their feet and ask them to try to find the conker/horse chestnut.

Materials

A conker/horse chestnut.
A selection of different natural materials such as a pebble, a leaf, a shell, some moss, and so on.

Whose Hat?

The group sit on chairs in a circle. One person closes their eyes. Three others line up closely next to each other. One of the three puts on a headscarf, the others put on different hats.

The person who has their eyes closed is led up to the three hat wearers and has to use their sense of touch to try to find out who is wearing the scarf.

Then roles are swapped to let others have a turn.

Materials

A headscarf and variety of other hats.

Mysterious Laundry Bag

Groups love this exercise, which can be played before tidying up at the end of the day. The exercise allows them to experience tidying up not as a 'tedious' chore, but as an enjoyable group game. To play the game, two group members at a time work together to place up to ten items in a laundry, or other large cloth, bag.

Now the game starts. While one person holds the laundry bag, the other reaches into the bag and takes hold of an item. While their hand is still inside the bag, they feels the object's shape and structure and then try to guess what it is.

To check whether they are right the object is taken out of the bag. If the guess is correct, the other person has to tidy away the object. If the guess is wrong, the guesser has to tidy it away themselves.

Materials

A laundry or large cloth bag.

Blowing Colourful Tracks

Young people love creating colourful patterns. This task requires groups to use marbles covered in paint to create blowing tracks that are as long as possible. In order for the members of the group to be able to distinguish between the different tracks, use a variety of different coloured finger or poster paints.

Ask everyone to stand in a relaxed manner with their piece of paper on the table, to carefully pick up a marble using only two fingers and then dip it into the paint of their choice.

Now ask them to place the marble on the paper and use a cloth to wipe their fingers.

Now get the group to take a deep breath and blow onto the marble. In order for the marble to leave as long a track as possible, the out-breath must be significantly longer than the in-breath.

Encourage everyone to breathe normally after each of these breaths to avoid feeling dizzy. Once they have had a 'breathing pause', ask them to repeat the exercise with a new coloured marble. At the end of the exercise, ask the group to carefully study the tracks they have made. Were there any particularly long exhalations indicated by telltale long coloured marble tracks?

Materials

Aprons, paper, cloth, marbles, a variety of coloured paints, small dishes.

Keep it in the Hoop

Ask the group to form pairs, and two at a time sit opposite each other on the floor. Between them place a hoop and a piece of cotton wool within the hoop.

The group's task is to blow at the piece of cotton wool to make it move, without blowing it out of the hoop. To do this everyone will have to carefully and precisely control their out-breath.

Before they start blowing the piece of cotton wool, encourage the group members to breathe out deeply and then take in a deep breath. They are not allowed to move from their places while they are blowing the piece of cotton wool.

Materials

A piece of cotton wool, one hoop for each pair.

Matchbox Slalom

Place six matchboxes on the table, one behind the other with a distance of approximately 10 cm between them.

One player starts by trying to blow a piece of cotton wool slalom-fashion around the matchboxes. This sounds easier than it is: in order to ensure that no matchboxes are blown over, players must work hard to slowly control and target their exhalations.

If someone blows over a matchbox, they are given a point. At the end, the winner is the player whose piece of cotton wool has reached the end of the obstacle course with the fewest points.

If the group are already well practised at this game, the obstacle blowing can be played under timed conditions or further matchboxes added.

Materials

Six matchboxes, a piece of cotton wool.

Feel the Air

All the group except one sit in a circle of chairs, close their eyes and hold out their hands. The remaining person is the 'wind child', whose task it is to walk as slowly and quietly as possible around the circle while the rest of the group remains still and quiet.

Eventually, the 'wind child' stops in front of someone, takes a deep breath and then slowly blows onto the outstretched hands of the other person. If that person senses the breath of air on their hands, they can open their eyes and in the next round, they become the 'wind child'.

Keep it in Your Hand

Ask each person to take a piece of cotton wool and place it on the palm of their flat hand.

Now ask everyone to take a long breath out so they can then breathe in more deeply using the diaphragm. When they come to breathe out again, ask them to use their out-breath to carefully and gently move the piece of cotton wool around on their hand. In order to ensure that cotton wool does not fall off their hand, the members of the group will have to concentrate and breathe out very evenly. As soon as they have finished their exhalation, ask them to pause and just breathe normally for a moment.

Then play again by getting the group to first take a long breath out and then breathe in deeply once again.

Afterwards, encourage the group to discuss their experiences during the game:

☼ How did they have to breathe out to move the piece of cotton wool around on their hand?

☼ What did the cotton wool feel like on their hand?

☼ Which other materials could be used for this exercise?

Materials

Cotton wool

Breath Walk

The group are going to go on a journey of discovery around the room.

Ask each person to walk slowly around the room and look for things that they can move using only their breath. Encourage them to breathe in deeply and then carefully control their exhalation while trying to make things move. If someone has found something that can be moved by breathing on it, they can share their discovery with the rest of the group, who can then have a go at using their own breath to make that item move.

Afterwards, the group can gather together to exchange experiences:

☼ Which items could be moved?

☼ What kind of materials were these items made off?

☼ What strategies did they use to increase the volume of their breath?

Leaf Vacuum Cleaner

Form the group into pairs and sit in their pairs on the floor in front of hoops.

In the middle of the hoop there are some leaves. Each person now has to try to pick up the leaves in the hoop by sucking them onto a straw.

Remind everyone to breathe out as much as possible each time before breathing in through the straw. This exercise requires a lot of concentration and so the group should be encouraged not to talk.

Materials

A variety of leaves
Straws
Hoops

Between Calm & Storm

Before starting the game, discuss with the group different wind speeds and agree different sounds to represent the various wind speeds. For example:

☀ Wind – clicking fingers

☀ A lull in the wind – rubbing hands together

☀ Storm – clapping hands and stamping feet

Now encourage everyone to think about which type of breath might correspond to the different wind speeds. While doing this, you can develop the following breathing techniques with the group:

☀ Wind – breathing out, taking a deep breath in and then slowly breathing out again

☀ Lull in the wind – calmly breathing out and back in again

☀ Storm – breathing out, taking a deep breath in and blowing out strongly

Once the different breathing techniques have been discussed and practised, use the previously agreed sounds to get the children to respond with the corresponding 'breathing wind'.

Table Football

Choose one person to be the referee. Form the remaining group members into two teams of equal size, sitting opposite each other at a table. At each end of the table create a goal from two building blocks or books. In the middle of the table place a piece of cotton wool.

As soon as the whistle is blown, both teams must try to blow the piece of cotton wool into their opponent's goal. If one team blows the piece of cotton wool off the table, the referee has to pick it up and place it in the middle of the table again. A 'free kick' is awarded to the other team.

After a previously agreed period of time, the whistle is blown again to signal the end of the game.

☼ Who blew the most goals?

Materials

Four building blocks or books
Cotton wool
Whistle

Don't Blow Over!

This exercise requires a high level of concentrated and controlled breathing. Give each member of the group a ball of cotton wool which they must carefully blow along the edge of the table without it falling over the edge.

To get ready for this exercise, ask everyone to take a deep breath in and then out again. Ask them to direct their out-breath onto the piece of cotton wool and practise blowing it slowly along the table, being careful not to blow it off the edge.

To prevent the group members from getting dizzy during this exercise, make sure that, after each targeted blow, they breathe normally for a short while.

The aim of the exercise is to blow the piece of cotton wool along the edge of the table using as few breaths as possible. In order to achieve this, the group members must increase their lung volume. They will only be able to do this if they carefully control their stream of breath and slowly breathe out, making each breath last for as long as possible.

Have you seen ...

3 Minute Motivators

More Than 100 Activities to Help you Reach, Teach and Achieve!

Kathy Paterson

This resource will show you how to turn around unmotivated, unfocused classes. With more than 100 practical and simple ideas that will refocus a group, release excess energy, or start a class with a bang.

Offering a wide variety of ready-to-use activities that turn potential problems into opportunities, and get pupils out of a rut and into a more productive mode:

- *Calm Down* – relaxing activities that let imaginations soar

- *Get Moving* – lively motivators

- *Act, Don't Speak* – silent but fun activities

- *Words and Movement* – activities that mix talk with action

- *Single Words & Sounds* – simple communication activities

- *Conversation* – getting motivated one-on-one

- *Brainstorms* – working together to let the ideas fly

- *Paper & pencil activities* – from letter and word play to shared stories.

An ideal resource for all teachers, teaching assistants and those running groups, promoting playful activities that involve competition, cooperation and opportunities to focus on real learning.

2009 • 172pp • paperback • 978-1-906531-00-3

Available from

Hinton House Publishers Ltd
Newman House, 4 High Street, Buckingham, MK18 1NT, UK
info@hintonpublishers.com
www.hintonpublishers.com

The 50 Best Group Games Pocket Books series

☼ These handy pocket books will ensure you are never again stuck for activity ideas that will help make both teaching and learning fun!

☼ Carefully selected, each collection of the 50 Best Games is themed and addresses a specific area of development. All the games are easy to implement with the minimum of preparation and can be adapted to the needs of your particular group.

☼ Use them as warm-ups, ice breakers, time fillers or to address a specific need. Suitable for groups of all sizes and can be used with all ages from young children to adolescents.

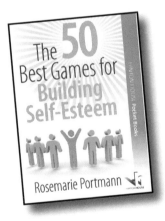

The 50 Best Games for Building Self-Esteem

Rosemarie Portmann

Help create self-confident children with these games for building strength and self-esteem. This selection of games will help improve self-awareness, assertiveness, and confidence as well as respect for others.

2008 • 64pp • ISBN 978-1-906531-18-8

Hinton House Publishers Ltd
Newman House, 4 High Street, Buckingham, MK18 1NT, UK
info@hintonpublishers.com
www.hintonpublishers.com

The 50 Best Games for Relaxation & Concentration

Rosemarie Portmann

Easy to use games to help your class relax and concentrate, with activities for reducing fidgeting, calming down, reflection, thinking and concentration.

2008 • 64pp • ISBN 978-1-906531-17-1

The 50 Best Games for Groups

Josef Griesbeck

All teachers and group leaders struggle to find suitable games from time to time. These themed activities will ensure you have a suitable game for any occasion – ice-breakers, closers, fun games, confidence builders and thinking games.

2009 • 64pp • ISBN 978-1-906531-16-4

Hinton House Publishers Ltd
Newman House, 4 High Street, Buckingham, MK18 1NT, UK
info@hintonpublishers.com
www.hintonpublishers.com

The 50 Best Games
for Children's Groups

Birgit Fuchs

Building group cohesion is not always easy. These fun games will enable children to feel part of the group and increase self-confidence, with activities that look at the individual, the group and communication skills.

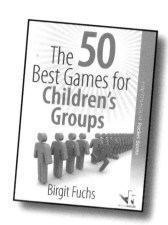

2009 • 64pp • ISBN 978-1-906531-12-6

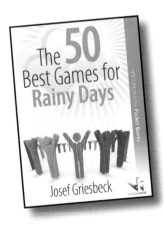

The 50 Best Games
for Rainy Days

Josef Griesbeck

Everyone working with children needs good, easily adaptable ideas for games. Never have that gloomy rainy day feeling again!

2009 • 64pp • ISBN 978-1-906531-15-7

Hinton House Publishers Ltd
Newman House, 4 High Street, Buckingham, MK18 1NT, UK
info@hintonpublishers.com
www.hintonpublishers.com